Difficult Customers

Grainne Ridge

D1492788

DIRECTORY OF SOCIAL CHANGE

Published by
Directory of Social Change
24 Stephenson Way
London NW1 2DP
Tel. 08450 77 77 07; Fax 020 7391 4804
email publications@dsc.org.uk
www.dsc.org.uk
from whom further copies and a full books catalogue are available.

Directory of Social Change is a Registered Charity no. 800517

First published 2011

ISBN 978 1 906294 21 2

British Library Cataloguing in Publication Data

A catalogue record for this book is available from the British Library

Cover and text designed by Kate Bass
Typeset by Marlinzo Services, Frome
Printed and bound by Martins the Printers, Berwick-upon-Tweed

All Directory of Social Change departments in London:
08450 77 77 07

Directory of Social Change Northern Office:
Research 0151 708 0136

For other titles in the DSC SPEED READ series go to:
www.dsc.org.uk/Publications/SpeedReadSeries

Contents

Introduction

Who is this book for?

This book will help those who want to feel more confident dealing with people who expect a service from them (such as funders, beneficiaries and volunteers). It is both a handbook for the inexperienced and a resource for more experienced people handlers who feel that they need a fresh perspective or a few more tools in their bag.

The logical, coaching structure and practical exercises lend themselves to team training sessions as well as to individual exploration.

What will it give you?

It will help you to build a positive approach to managing these relationships and show you how to set yourself apart. You can develop a strategic plan for your organisation. You can use this book to guide you in developing a complete customer service strategy for your organisation, or you may simply choose to adopt the top tips and tools in the areas where you have the greatest challenges.

Chapter 1

Who are the customers?

In this chapter you will look at what makes a 'customer' in your organisation, uncover the expectations that they have of you and your service, and create a distinct and positive customer experience plan.

Definition and scope within the voluntary sector

It is inherently difficult to find a word that accurately represents all recipients of services within the voluntary sector. For you it may be 'client', 'beneficiary', 'stakeholder' or 'funder'. We recognise that it would be unwieldy and confusing to use these interchangeably, so for the purposes of this book, we have settled on 'customer'. It is probably the most generic and understood word to refer to any of these recipients without attaching any commercial connotations.

When thinking about *your* customers, decide who you have the greatest level of contact with and who see you directly as a provider.

Now consider who your customers are.

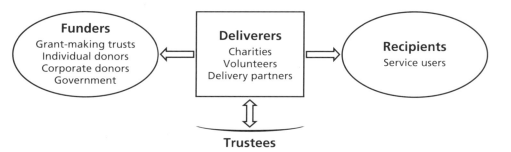

Make a list like the one below to help you determine who your customers are.

Who are your funders?	Who benefits from your services?
For example: general public	For example: people living with cancer

What makes a valuable relationship?

Each customer will value their relationship with you in different ways. This could include valuing service, mutual benefit, satisfaction, enjoyment, value for money, new ideas, feedback, learning or problem solving. What is important then is that you consider what the customer really wants. Do they simply need you to provide information or a practical service? Do they want to feel involved and valued? Do they need to be guided step by step through a process that is new and daunting to them?

Why 'customer experience' is important in this sector

Every customer who deals with your organisation will be able to say what it is like to deal with you. This definition will reflect all of their experiences, including:

- how the phone is answered
- how quickly you understood what they needed
- the quality of the information that you provided
- the way in which you provided it
- how they were dealt with when they complained.

They will be able to say, 'Dealing with Charity X is...' What words will they put in this gap? See the case study for an example.

Whether your customers are spending time or money with your organisation, they will expect to receive value in return. They will want to feel that they have made a good decision. Each good experience they have with you will build loyalty and trust. In the case of funders this could mean continuing investment, and for service users it could be life-changing support.

Existing customers are often our best advocates. However, if they have had a bad experience they are even more likely to talk about it!

Problem-solving is at the heart of the voluntary sector, so use those situations where you have dealt successfully with a difficult customer complaint to demonstrate and reinforce positive perceptions of your skills and service.

Practical analysis of your customer relationships

In order to provide a consistently good customer experience it is important to know how well you currently perform. Let's look at this compared to what you set out to do, for whom and how.

Step 1

Identify your groups of customers (see p. 6).

Case study

When I spoke to Action Against Poverty they were so calm and reassuring. On the phone they suggested things I could do now to stop the situation getting worse. The information they sent me was really easy to understand. I had been very upset at first, so they phoned the local support group and got them to contact me.

Top tip

Try writing down for yourself what you think it is like for customers dealing with your organisation.

Step 2

Find out what your customers want or need from you:

- Ask a broad selection of them.
- Ask them to rank these needs in importance.
- Decide, from their priorities, how many needs you can fulfil.

For example: a corporate donor you spoke to has said that they commit to report monthly to their board on their charitable donations. They want to see income and expenditure figures, specifically to understand what percentage of income reaches the service users. In addition, they would like case studies illustrating how individuals have benefited, and once a year they would like your chief executive to meet with them and present on the charity's five-year plans. To meet their reporting timescales, the monthly information would need to be with them by the 24th of every month.

As a relatively small charity you do not have the resources to collate all of this information every month, so you propose to report quarterly. You also believe that creating plans for years 4 and 5 would be time-consuming and of little value, as the service users' needs and the social factors could have changed significantly. However, you do plan three years ahead. The donor understands your constraints and accepts your proposed reporting timescales.

Step 3

What are the characteristics of your service as your customers would describe them? For example:

'They are very creative in the way that they solve problems.'

'They were so welcoming.'

'They pay great attention to detail so that the information we receive is always accurate and timely.'

Top tip

Create a feedback process where you encourage converted 'difficult customers' to a forum to post a positive statement.

Top tip

If you can't fulfil an important need, explain this to your customer in the early stages of the relationship rather than hoping that they won't notice. Set out what is achievable and deliver without fail on this.

'They always do what they say they will, no matter who it is you speak to in the organisation.'

How do your customers describe your service?

Step 4

This is the results stage: how well do you deliver what you set out to deliver? Compare the customer feedback captured in step 3 with the needs and wants of your customers in step 2, and create a table as follows.

Top tip

When you ask for feedback, be prepared to hear the bad or ugly as well as the good: the bad will be the most useful.

What we do well	What else is important to our customers?	How could we meet those needs?

One way in which you could use such a template is within a customer service improvement session with your team or, better still, with a group drawn from across the full range of functions within the organisation. Once you have set a precedent with your customers for gathering feedback, keep doing it.

Not only will the process of asking for feedback give you valuable information, and a more balanced view than the *ad hoc* comments from satisfied or dissatisfied customers, it will:

■ give you the opportunity to reinforce those good customer service characteristics that you have worked hard to deliver;

■ set you apart as an organisation that really wants to listen; and most crucially

■ pre-empt and avoid potential customer complaints.

Top tip

The very best organisations don't just treat customer service as part of what they do – customers are their reason for being.

**Mike Phillips,
Trainer and
Consultant**

Chapter 2

Difficult behaviour

This chapter will help you identify the situations you find most difficult and show you how to influence customers' expectations.

Why does difficult behaviour happen?

A customer that we see as difficult may be angry, challenging, unclear about what they want, abusive, demanding an excessive amount of our time, and possibly never satisfied, no matter how much we try.

When we start to see a customer as difficult it can be challenging ever to see them as anything other than difficult. By putting yourself in the customers' shoes you can understand why they might be acting in this way:

Difficult behaviour	Standing in their shoes
Angry	'They didn't call when they said they would', or 'I need someone to blame'
Challenging	'I need a quick response so that I can help my client who has an urgent need'
Unclear	'I need some help but I'm not sure what is on offer'
Abusive	'They have no idea how frustrating it is to be passed from pillar to post'
Excessively demanding	'I like lots of detail and to feel involved'

The point of standing in the customer's shoes is to help us to understand their perspective. All difficult behaviour has a purpose. It may be that the customer needs information urgently, or they want you to know that they are unhappy. When you show people that you understand how they feel, you start to build or rebuild the relationship. This is the first step in solving the underlying issue.

Within the voluntary sector, there can be additional tensions. Often there will be a range of parties involved in each cause: funders, providers, volunteers and service users. Each may believe that they are experts, although they have different contributions to make. Recognising and valuing the differences in these contributions is a starting point for defusing tension and alleviating difficult behaviour.

How much can we influence?

Customers all have an expectation of the service that they should receive from us. When the reality falls short of this, this is when we often experience difficult behaviour. Which of these can we influence – the expectation or the reality?

The answer, of course, is both.

Five ways to influence customer expectations

1 Communicate what you do and how you do it.
2 Give them a good or bad experience of your service.
3 Encourage other people to talk about what you do.
4 Work with customers to understand what they need and agree how best to deliver it.
5 Surprise them by unexpectedly sending something relevant to them.

'Customer reality' is defined as what they actually experience – not what we think we have delivered. For

Top tip

Consider and make a list of the behaviours you find difficult, then stand in your customers' shoes and decide why they might be acting in this way.

Top tip

All behaviour has meaning. Think of some recent examples of difficult behaviour you have faced. What might be the reasons behind this behaviour?

Mike Phillips, Trainer and Consultant

11

example, we may think that we have created a useful website with all the information that our customers could possibly need, including links to other services, but if they cannot find what they want, we haven't delivered exactly what they need.

Creating realistic expectations

What do we set out to do? Is it:

- to help those living in poverty in the UK?
- to provide housing for every homeless person?
- to help people to take control of their mental health?
- to provide practical support to families with sick children?
- to do the best we can with the money we have?

Sometimes our cause can be extremely ambitious and this, in turn, can create very high expectations from our customers. Breaking our purpose down into manageable chunks helps us to communicate clearly what our customers can expect and limit the incidence of dissatisfied or 'difficult' customers.

It might be helpful to list what your organisation sets out to do, followed by what each of your customers can realistically expect from you (see the table on p. 13 for examples).

Now go back to the five ways in which you can influence expectations. Decide how you will ensure that your customers know what they can expect, and how you currently deliver against these.

Examples

Charity objective	Realistic expectations
To help those living in poverty in the UK	■ To be the first point of contact for individuals who are living in poverty and lead them to the best next step ■ To guide individuals in the process of accessing all the benefits available to them
To provide practical support for families with sick children	■ To provide someone to coordinate accommodation for parents who live more than 15 miles from the hospital ■ To run sibling clubs to support children aged between 3 and 12 whose siblings are seriously ill.

Which behaviours are difficult for you?

Now think about which types of behaviour you find difficult: perhaps only some of the common problematic behaviours trigger the feeling of a difficult situation for you. By considering the following questions you can start to isolate them and to work out how to manage these difficult situations.

■ Which customers do you find most difficult to deal with?

■ For each of these, which type of behaviour do you find difficult to deal with?

■ What could you do to limit the situations that prompt this behaviour?

■ What else would help to limit these situations?

■ Which difficult behaviours do you manage well?

Top tip

Become aware of who you manage well and how. These strategies may be applicable elsewhere.

Chapter 3

Useful mindsets

This chapter explains the importance of mindsets in dealing with your customers, how to adopt the most powerful ones, and how to maintain these when the going gets tough.

The impact of our mindsets

The way in which we perceive our ability to manage difficult behaviour will affect what we do in practice and, in turn, will affect the results we get.

Think of your different types of customer.

Get **See**

Do

- Do you feel equally confident dealing with each, or are you more confident with some than with others? This is the 'see' part of the model.
- Do you behave the same with each, or does this vary depending on how you see them?
- Do you get the same results with each?

We can see this model at work in all aspects of our life. When we see ourselves as being in control and confident we are effective in what we do and we get good results. Compare this to a situation where we don't feel confident or in control, or when faced with someone who we see as difficult.

As the model is circular, we can change what we do to get different results – which, in turn, will affect our perceptions.

How are we using our mindsets to help or hinder?

The label 'difficult' itself is unhelpful in equipping us to deal with each situation. Much more useful is the practice of separating the person from the problem: immediately we start to see the situation differently. For example, the angry customer is someone who is angry because they have not had the service they expected.

When we find ourselves thinking, 'Oh here we go again, a difficult one', or we feel we are being attacked, we physically and mentally set ourselves up to expect a difficult situation. What happens?

- Our muscles tense.
- Our breath becomes shorter.
- We stop smiling and probably frown.
- We can only see what is in front of us and become less able to think of solutions.

When these physical changes occur we are less able to deal with the difficult behaviour. The good news is that we can consciously affect our physical and mental states and, thereby, our capacity to deal with the situation.

Creating powerful mindsets

The voluntary sector exists fundamentally to support people with a wide range of problems. Solving or alleviating these is at the heart of what it does. A 'difficult customer' is another person with a problem, so adopting this starting point will be helpful.

Remember:

- you will have some commonality in your goals or shared goals

---

Top tip

Remember that 'difficult' customers help us to see the gaps in our service. They are the ones who point out what isn't working and what needs to happen instead. Are you using this valuable feedback to improve your service?

Shireen Mustafa-Johal, Head of Customer Services and Facilities, DSC

Top tip

It can be helpful to think of customer complaints as a gift and the layers of paper as what you unwrap to get to the reasons beneath the complaint. Some gifts we receive may not be wanted but we still need to acknowledge and appreciate them.

Mike Phillips, Trainer and Consultant

- they would not be contacting you if they didn't think you could do something about it
- you have been given an opportunity to turn their experience into a good one
- you will have solved people's problems previously and can do it again.

Think of some recent situations where you had to deal with an angry, challenging, excessively demanding customer – or any other difficult behaviour you can think of.

Which of these mindsets applied to you?	Which would have been more helpful?
'She's very important and will think I'm useless.'	'I have all of the information I need and have the opportunity to shine.'
'They're out to get me.'	'This is an individual situation and I have dealt with this before.'
'He's angry with me.'	'He is angry about the situation rather than me.'
'They're never satisfied.'	'What specifically can I do to resolve this issue?'
'I don't know what to do.'	'I can take it step by step, starting with listening.'

Think of some more examples where your mindset was unhelpful, and what would have been a more resourceful one.

Ways to get into a resourceful state

Visualisation

It works for top performers in many areas, including sports and business, and it can work for you too.

Think of a time at work when you were completely in control. Remember the sounds in the office. Who was nearby? How did you sound: calm and happy, clear, sympathetic and sincere? How did you feel: bright and alert, calm, like you were enjoying yourself? Keep building the picture and notice how you now start to feel as you did then.

When you have the most complete picture of being in control, squeeze the top of your thumb with your forefinger! Repeat the process five times, squeezing your thumb and forefinger just at the point where the image and feeling is strongest and hold the squeeze for about 10 seconds. This is the start of the Neuro-Linguistic Programming (NLP) process of 'anchoring', where you can instantly recreate a positive state that will help you deal with a difficult situation.

Replacing negative triggers

Have you ever found yourself thinking, 'I am not going to get upset when ... '? We have identified that there is a trigger that tends to set off a negative response within ourselves. It may be, for example, that hearing the voice of a particular volunteer on the phone puts you on edge and you expect to hear of another shortcoming they have identified with your information packs.

Setting out not to get upset in this situation won't work. Our brains aren't good at *not* doing things. A more effective technique is to think about how you want to respond and to create a very vivid picture of the positive response, for example: 'When I hear Libby's voice I will see both of us smiling, I will say how good it is to speak to her again, and I will feel interested in what she has to say.'

It takes practice to change your automatic responses. The starting point is to recognise patterns in your responses that get in the way of your capacity to deal with difficult behaviour.

Where next?

Neuro-linguistic Programming Workbook for Dummies, Romilla Ready and Kate Burton, John Wiley & Sons, 2008.

Introducing NLP Neuro-Linguistic Programming, Joseph O'Connor and John Seymour, Thorsons, 2003.

Where next?

Association for Neuro-Linguistic Programming, the independent voice for NLP: www.anlp.org

Businessballs on NLP: tinyurl.com/businessballs-nlp

Where next?

For more advice on stress management techniques, see: www.mindtools.com

Top tip

Every experience teaches us – even the bad ones. We learn how to do it better and it builds confidence in our ability to handle difficult behaviour.

Mike Phillips, Trainer and Consultant

Breathing

When a situation makes us feel tense our breathing becomes shallow, and this isn't useful. Practice the 'sigh' technique to instantly reduce your tension levels.

- Breathe in slowly and evenly through your nose. (This is a moderate breath in, rather than a deep one.)
- Pause for a second and then let the air out very slowly through your nose.
- As you breathe out, relax your shoulders, face, jaw and abdomen.

Don't worry, your customer won't be hearing heavy breathing! You will feel less anxious now and ready to deal with the situation.

Abusive behaviour

You don't have to put up with abusive behaviour. When a customer speaks or behaves in a threatening way they are normally looking for a reaction from you that will justify their bad behaviour. So, what should you do?

- Stay calm (see 'Breathing' above).
- State the consequences – for example, 'I can't help you while you are shouting at me. If you continue, I will hang up.'
- If they continue to be abusive, follow through with the consequences (if they have calmed down, apply the seven-step process set out in Chapter 5, see p. 26).

It can be very unsettling to experience abusive behaviour and it could affect your confidence in future situations. If you do find it that affects how you feel at work, talk it through with a colleague or your manager.

Remember the different ways that you can get back into a resourceful state – practise them so that they become second nature.

Chapter 4

Pre-emptive tactics

This chapter looks at practical ways to limit the incidences of customer complaints, leaving you with enough energy to tackle those unavoidable challenges.

How to create strong relationships

Understanding what is important to your customer, aligning your services with this and then delivering against expectations is at the heart of a good customer relationship. However, each issue or problem can undermine it. What else can we do to strengthen the relationship so that it weathers any storms?

Five ways to make customers feel valued

1   Ask their advice on a new service or way of working.
2   Talk about their support in your public relations, if they are happy to be included.
3   Thank them without asking for more money.
4   Send them free updates or information that you know they will find useful.
5   Change the way that you do things, based on their feedback.

Where next?

Use www.survey monkey.com to create and manage free online customer feedback.

Is this different for different customers?

It can help to think about each of your groups of customers and generate some ways that you can strengthen the relationship with each. Below are some general ideas to help get you started.

Funders	Deliverers	Service users
■ Clear contracts ■ Regular updates and reviews ■ Recognition	■ Recognition and awards ■ Project collaboration ■ Regular communication	■ Involve them in a customer service improvement panel ■ Communicate the difference that they have made

How to be proactive

The events which lead to customer complaints come from one of three areas:

■ individual employees
■ the organisation
■ the customer.

Where next?

Keeping Volunteers, **Steve McCurley and Rick Lynch, 2007, DSC.**

With this in mind, what can we do to pre-empt these complaints and thereby reduce the number of them?

Make a list like the one overleaf and score each of these statements on a scale of 1–10, where 1 is poor and 10 is excellent, in each of these areas.

Improving your scores in each of these areas will have a direct impact on the customer service that you can deliver.

Individual employees	Score
They know your products and services	
They know the people in your organisation and how each of them can help deliver customer service	
They understand and use all of the processes and technology effectively to deliver an excellent service	
They know how best to communicate with each customer	
The organisation	
It delivers a high quality of services (such as advice, information, training, conferences, books)	
It recognises the value of customer services	
It communicates with its customers so they know what they can expect	
It handles complaints effectively	
The customer	
They know how best to use your services	

Best practice in dealing with mistakes

Checklist

- ❏ Be aware of timing and act quickly. Make sure you use the quickest form of communication.
- ❏ Apologise for what has happened and for the impact that the mistake has had on the customer.
- ❏ Research the options: before you contact the customer, consider a variety of ways that might solve the issue.

Case study

A supermarket delivery service is recognised as being the best in the sector, with an order fulfilment level of more than 99%. It pre-empts issues to minimise complaints and create customer advocates. In the ordering process, it offers alternatives if the customer's choice is unavailable. If items become unavailable, it lets customers know in advance of the substitutions. If they don't like the substitution, it removes it and refunds with no quibble. If the order is extremely late, the service has been known to waive the total cost of the shopping.

❑ Understand the issues: ask them which options would work best, or what else needs to happen.
❑ Consider compensation: this needs to be seen as high value to the customer and yet might be low cost to you.

Joined-up customer service

We all know how frustrating it is to be handed from pillar to post and to have to explain who we are and what we want several times over. As customers we want to get straight to the person who can help us. If we don't succeed, the next best solution is to be handed over seamlessly to someone who can help. What needs to be in place in your organisation to make this happen?

Checklist

❑ Full customer details are taken by the first point of contact.
❑ Customer details are recorded systematically and are easily accessible.
❑ If the customer is handed over, details of them and their enquiry are communicated by the first point of contact to the second contact.
❑ The customer is greeted personally by the second contact and their enquiry and progress to date summarised.
❑ Your operative provides their direct contact details in case the customer has further questions.
❑ It is absolutely clear what each person in the organisation is responsible for.
❑ There is clear communication to customers on who to contact for each element of your services.
❑ If an automated answering service is used, the pre-selected services are clearly defined, reflecting what customers are most likely to need.

Building customer advocates

Customer advocates are particularly powerful, as they will spread the message of your great customer service and reinforce the value of what you offer. In turn, this could help a dissatisfied customer to believe that their experience was unusual rather than typical.

How can you harness customer advocates?

- Encourage your happy customers to provide testimonials.
- Email your converted customers and ask for testimonials: endorsements from these customers are often more powerful.
- Direct them to a forum where they can talk of their great experiences.
- Involve them in an ongoing customer care programme: e.g. make follow-up calls to check customer satisfaction and gather their views on your services.

Where next?

Customer Genius, P Fisk, Capstone, 2009.

Case study

Never Again International, a non-profit network dedicated to promoting peace and preventing genocide, has members throughout the world, with chapters in Burundi, Canada, China, Rwanda, the United Kingdom and the United States. With so many people dispersed around the globe, the organisation needed a way to communicate, centralise information and ease collaboration. Never Again's communications coordinator Clare-Marie White said:

> *Because we are scattered it is very difficult to know what [members] don't know, so we really need ways of sharing knowledge when people travel.*

To overcome this obstacle, Never Again International adopted a wiki: neveragain.epov.org/Main_Page.

23

Case study

Your organisation committed to help a charity with a funding application. Their case was strong. However, your adviser missed a key appointment. The charity missed the deadline, and consequently got no funding: they are angry and upset. You immediately apologise and commit to call in half an hour with a full explanation. You investigate and research other sources of funding. You call back at the agreed time, say what you have done to stop this happening again, and detail the alternative funding. You offer to work with them today to complete the application, and arrange for a senior manager to call the next day to check they are happy with the solution.

Delivering against expectations

This should be easy if you know what your customers need and you have aligned your resources to deliver. Use this checklist to rate how you are doing at the moment, to keep on track and to identify any areas that need fixing.

Checklist

- ❏ Get customers' names and details right.
- ❏ Deliver on time and in full.
- ❏ Keep communicating.
- ❏ Provide accurate information.
- ❏ Act promptly when a mistake has been made.
- ❏ Suggest links to additional resources.
- ❏ Know your products and services.
- ❏ Know how your organisation works.
- ❏ Make it easy for customers to give feedback.
- ❏ Act on feedback.

Exceeding expectations

Most organisations set out only to meet expectations, thereby leaving themselves little leeway for failure. Why not aim higher and give yourself the chance to exceed expectations? When a customer has a surprisingly good experience of your service they are more likely to become valuable advocates, and we have seen how they can assist us in dealing with dissatisfied customers.

As you consistently exceed expectations you create a new standard against which your customers will measure you. Remember to build these new improved processes into your organisation's way of working.

However, having done everything you can to pre-empt those difficult situations, there will still be occasions when 'difficult customers' surface.

Chapter 5

Practical approaches

This chapter will arm you with approaches that you can use in the moment to turn 'difficult customers' into satisfied customers or even advocates.

A step-by-step process

It is hard to be cross with someone when you are in rapport, so how can you create and maintain rapport? You can affect it immediately through your language, using the same words and phrases, and speaking with the same tone and at the same speed as the other person. Your body language has an even bigger impact than your words. How well listened to do you feel when someone continues to read while you are talking to them? In the longer term you strengthen rapport through your behaviour – doing what you say you will do.

However, when confronted by difficult behaviour it can be hard not to respond emotionally and, in so doing, to inflame the situation. The following process will help you to separate the problem from the emotion. It builds in time for you to manage your feelings so that you can be resourceful, and shows the other person that you want to understand and resolve the issue, even if it is their mistake. Remember, no one ever won an argument with a customer!

Where next?

NLP at Work: The Essence of Excellence, **S Knight, Nicholas Brealey Publishing, 2009.**

1 Listen.
2 Question to fully understand the issue.
3 Apologise for or acknowledge the bad experience they have had.
4 Recap your understanding of the issue, using their words – if they aren't abusive.
5 Suggest options to resolve the issue.
6 Ask which of these options would work best for them.
7 Confirm the actions which will resolve the issue.

Where next?

DSC runs a course on excellence in customer care. To find out more go to: www.dsc.org.uk/customercare

The importance of step 1 – allowing your customer to vent their anger, frustration or dissatisfaction without interruption and while showing that you are listening – cannot be overstated. Until they have had the opportunity to tell you what is wrong, they will not be even slightly interested in what you have to say.

In step 2 you get a speaking part, but only to dig deeper into the issue. Importantly, your questions will be uncovering all of the facts and not just building up the case for your defence.

When steps 1 and 2 are done well, you will sense that your customer is now receptive to what you have to say. Step 3 is your opportunity to show them that you are on their side, and in step 4 you get to prove your excellent listening skills. Fine tuning your joint understanding of the issue by recapping means that you are more likely to make appropriate suggestions – you wouldn't want to rekindle their dissatisfaction with an inappropriate 'one size fits all' suggestion.

What if you don't know how to resolve the issue?

Here is an example.

You have just started working in the accounts team of a charity which provides activities for children in deprived urban areas. An angry donor has phoned, apparently for the fifth time, to complain that their direct debits have been taken out twice for the last three months. They now want to cancel their contributions completely. You are not sure exactly where to start to resolve this issue.

Your first objective is to keep them as a donor. They will need a good experience of your organisation to change their negative perception. After having listened and questioned to understand (the first two steps), this is how you could use and expand on the subsequent steps to start to rebuild their commitment:

'I am very new to the organisation but I will do my best to help you. I completely understand why you are so unhappy with this situation and I would feel the same if I were you. I need to speak to a colleague and I will come back to you with an update within one hour.'

Even if you don't have the final answer, make sure you return that call within the hour. Remember that you can use other people with more experience in your organisation to help you resolve customer complaints.

Using language to help

It is so easy to say the wrong thing, or the right thing in the wrong way. The power of language is in using it to create a sense of a shared problem which you are now going to fix.

Key rules about effective language

- Use 'we' rather than 'you'.
- Avoid 'but', as it signals that you disagree.
- Apologise for what they have experienced – not necessarily for what you have done, if you haven't actually made a mistake.
- Use the customer's words, if they are not abusive.

Don't say:	Do say:
'It states clearly in our terms...'	'What we aim to do is...'
'You put the wrong information in'	'It looks as though the address is wrong'
'You didn't send us the application'	'If you could send it to us today, we will...'
'You misunderstood'	'It can be ambiguous'
'You are being difficult'	'Let's try to sort this out'
'Just calm down'	'I can hear that you're very upset and I would like to help'

Even more important than the specific words that the very best communicators use is how they say those words: the tone. This includes the speed, pitch and volume of people's voices. If our unhappy customer is rattling out cross words at a great pace and we respond in a slow drawl, they are likely to interpret our response as uninterested. However, overtly copying the other person's tone characteristics is not advisable – aim to move closer to their way of speaking.

Creative solutions

Compensation

Compensation is not about throwing money or freebies at unhappy customers in the hope that they will be placated. Most will want a solution to their issue, and only some will expect some form of recompense.

However, it is worth considering the role of compensation in the customer experience that you set out to deliver (see p. 6). For example, do you set out to compensate not just for the value of the product but for the customer's bad experience?

Here are some examples of compensation that your organisation could offer:

Top tip

Remember that the key rule on compensation is that it *must* be seen to be valuable by the customer.

Shireen Mustafa-Johal, Head of Customer Services and Facilities, DSC

- a free place at the next conference
- an additional publication
- half-price membership for a second person in their organisation
- a phone call from someone very senior in your organisation
- a letter of apology
- your time to help them with an application.

Think of the customer complaints you have dealt with and what form of compensation would have worked best.

Using other people

Below is a list of situations when it might be a good idea – or indeed necessary – to involve others in your organisation in order to help with a dissatisfied customer:

- you don't know the answer
- you are too upset to deal with them
- they need reassurance
- your proposals don't satisfy them
- you will not have time to solve the problem.

The seven-step process will be very effective in supporting you. However, it is important to recognise when you are not best placed to solve the problem. If you get to step 4 and realise that you need help, be prepared to hand the customer over, using the best practice discussed on p. 21.

Engaging the customer

If they know so much about how things should be done around here, then why not involve them in the solution! This could range from a simple question to a full-blown meeting. Consider these options in increasing range of investment by the customer. Ask them:

'What can I do to put this right for you?'

'From the options you have listed, which would be best for you?'

'What do you feel we should do differently to improve the process?'

'Would you be prepared to spend time separately talking to us about how to improve our service in future?'

'We would be so grateful if you would join our customer service excellence panel.'

The first two in the above list can be very useful in curtailing customers who have a tendency to keep talking, or who want to share an immense amount of details.

Hands on deck

Think of a time when you have been that 'difficult customer'. Most people find that recollecting their experiences with phone and other utility services can recreate that sense of frustration and even draw out real tears. Now think of how it would have felt had the person dealing with your issue resolved it as you spoke – it might be too hard to imagine. There is little more disarming than a quick and complete solution.

Let's go back to your difficult customer situations. When the challenge seems big, decide on the following things.

- What can I do now that would help?
- What do I need to take away to resolve?

This will help you to feel more in control while demonstrating to your customer that you are taking their issue seriously. It is also useful in separating the emotion from the problem.

Chapter 6

Let me at 'em!

This chapter will lead you through a review of the book to identify the key things that you can implement to pre-empt and handle difficult customer situations.

Your plan

Pre-emptive actions

- You understand what your customers value in the relationship.
- Everyone in your organisation understands how they can deliver the best customer experience.
- You recognise the contribution that different customers bring to your cause.
- As an organisation you are much clearer on the scope of what you offer to your range of customers.
- You have strategies to make clear what customers can expect from you.

In-the-moment actions

- The seven-step process is understood and used by everyone in your organisation.
- A list of knowledge experts in the organisation is readily accessible on your system.
- Everyone has been trained in using stress management techniques, such as breathing, visualisation and triggers.
- The team has created a compensation policy and new creative options are added regularly.

■ A culture of positive and resourceful mindsets means that people see 'difficult customers' as something that they are good at managing.

Aftercare

■ Good customer service is measured and openly communicated in your organisation.

■ You celebrate successes in team and organisation meetings, such as problems being resolved.

■ A customer panel meets three times each year to review customer needs. This feeds into discussions on strategy.

Which of these will help you to deliver an improved service to your customers? Which will make your job more enjoyable? They may be the same for each.

How to keep on track

Now you have put all the effort into improving your approach, make it last with ideas from each of these areas. It might help to use a table such as this to generate ideas that would work best in your organisation.

Feedback loops	Recognition
■ Record all complaints and review why they happened and how they were resolved ■ Survey your customers at least once a year (this may need some incentive)	■ Propose a customer service award for handling difficult customer situations well ■ Communicate measures internally and testimonials externally
Support	**Confidence building**
■ Run a best practice sharing session with your team or organisation ■ Talk through difficult situations with a colleague or manager	■ Keep a record of your successes ■ Ask for feedback